A Note to P

DK READERS is a compelling progra... ... ...g ...ders, designed in conjunction with leading literacy experts, including Dr. Linda Gambrell, Distinguished Professor of Education at Clemson University. Dr. Gambrell has served as President of the National Reading Conference, the College Reading Association, and the International Reading Association.

Beautiful illustrations and superb full-color photographs combine with engaging, easy-to-read stories to offer a fresh approach to each subject in the series. Each DK READER is guaranteed to capture a child's interest while developing his or her reading skills, general knowledge, and love of reading.

The five levels of DK READERS are aimed at different reading abilities, enabling you to choose the books that are exactly right for your child:

Pre-level 1: Learning to read
Level 1: Beginning to read
Level 2: Beginning to read alone
Level 3: Reading alone
Level 4: Proficient readers

The "normal" age at which a child begins to read can be anywhere from three to eight years old. Adult participation through the lower levels is very helpful for providing encouragement, discussing storylines, and sounding out unfamiliar words.

No matter which level you select, you can be sure that you are helping your child learn to read, then read to learn!

LONDON, NEW YORK, MUNICH,
MELBOURNE, and DELHI

Series Editor Deborah lock
US Senior Editor Shannon Beatty
Project Art Editor Hoa Luc
Production Editor Francesca Wardell
Illustrator Hoa Luc

Reading Consultant
Linda Gambrell, Ph.D.

DK DELHI
Editor Pomona Zaheer
Art Editor Shruti Soharia Singh
DTP Designer Anita Yadav
Picture Researcher Aditya Katyal
Deputy Managing Editor Soma B. Chowdhury

First American Edition, 2014
Published in the United States by DK Publishing
345 Hudson Street, New York, New York 10014

14 15 16 17 10 9 8 7 6 5 4 3 2 1
001-195864-February/2014

A catalog record for this book is available
from the Library of Congress.

ISBN: 978-1-4654-1719-0 (Paperback)
ISBN: 978-1-4654-1919-4 (Hardcover)

DK books are available at special discounts when purchased in bulk for
sales promotions, premiums, fund-raising, or educational use.
For details, contact:
DK Publishing Special Markets
345 Hudson Street, New York, New York 10014
SpecialSales@dk.com

Printed and bound in China by
South China Printing Company

The publisher would like to thank the following for their kind
permission to reproduce their photographs:
(Key: a=above, b=below/bottom, c=center, l=left, r=right, t=top)
2 Fotolia: Adrio (br). 3 Dreamstime.com: Dragoneye (cra); Fotolia:
Proma (c). 4 Getty Images: Nigel Pavitt / AWL Images (b).
5 Dreamstime.com: Aughty Venable (t). 9 Stu Porter (tr).
10–11 Dreamstime.com: Alextara (background). 11 Corbis: Katie
Garrod / Jai (br). 15 Alamy Images: Richard Garvey-Williams (t),
Corbis: Barry Lewis / In Pictures (b). 23 Dorling Kindersley: Rough
Guides (t). 25 Getty Images: Sune Wendelboe / Lonely Planet Images (t).
33 Dreamstime.com: Richard Carey (t). 34 Corbis: Jami Tarris (t);
Dreamstime.com: Martesia Bezuidenhout (b). 36 Corbis: Gallo Images
(b). 37 Getty Images: AFP (t); Dreamstime.com: Hedrus (br).
40 Dreamstime.com: Sandra Van Der Steen. 42 Corbis: Jake Warga
(bl). 43 Corbis: Dlillc (br); Antony Njuguna / X90056 / Reuters (tc).
44 Dreamstime.com: Daleen Loest (cb). 45 Corbis: Martin Harvey (t).
Jacket images: Back cover © Herbert Kehrer / Imagebroker / Corbis
All other images © Dorling Kindersley
For further information see: www.dkimages.com

Discover more at
www.dk.com

Contents

4   My Safari Diary

6   Day 1

10   African Antelopes

16   The World Tree

18   Day 2

26   Day 3

32   Day 4

38   Day 5

42   Maasai Village

46   Glossary

47   Index

DK READERS

READING
3
ALONE

African Adventure

Written by Deborah Lock

My Safari Diary

I am now settled into camp. We have been traveling for two days. The best part of our long flight was flying over the snow-capped Mount Kenya. After landing in Nairobi, we had a three-hour bumpy jeep trip.

Mount Kenya

We have already seen some large birds. There were marabou storks on the edge of the towns. They are ugly!

I am very excited about this week. I wonder if I will get to see all of the Big Five: the lion, African elephant, Cape buffalo, leopard, and rhinoceros.

Day 1

6:00 AM Breakfast

6:30 AM Game drive

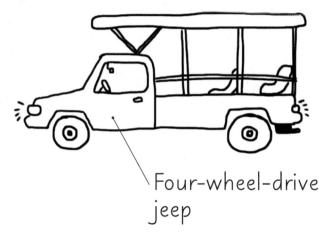

Four-wheel-drive jeep

12:00 noon Lunch

1:30 PM River trip

7:00 PM Dinner and
        campfire stories

I have just had a quick rest. Our morning game drive was worth the early start though. There were many animals roaming the savannah before the heat of the day.

Gazelles and the small dik-diks grazed among the herds of zebras and wildebeest. There are millions of zebras and wildebeest in this area at this time of year. They will stay a month or two to eat before migrating on.

Zebras and wildebeest on the move.
Watch out behind you!

Fastest big cat

A cheetah has a top speed of 64 mph (102 kph), which makes it not only the fastest-moving of all big cats, but also of all land animals.

We watched a cheetah. She had killed an impala but was letting her cubs feed first. Giraffes strutted proudly, stopping to nibble at the thornbushes. It is amazing how close we can get to these animals in our jeep.

African Antelopes

Here's a field guide to identifying some of the many types of antelope found in the savannah.

1. Gerenuk
Spot by its long neck and long legs. The male has thick, ringed horns.

2. Topi
Spot this medium-size antelope by the dark patches on its face and its upper legs.

3. Thomson's gazelle
Look out for the black stripes on its face and sides.

4. Dik-dik

A small antelope that has large dark marks within a white ring around its eyes.

5. Greater kudu

Look out for the white stripes on its body and the line of white between its eyes. The male has long spiral horns.

6. Gemsbok

Males and females have long, spear-like horns. Also look out for the black-and-white markings on their faces and legs.

We spent the afternoon on the river. We saw crocodiles basking in the sun on the muddy riverbanks. They looked scary with their mouths open.

We came across a few hippo pods, too. Hippos are huge but most of the time you can only see the top of their heads. They peer over the water plants. Each time, our guide slowed the boat and kept a safe distance away. He knew the danger. Hippos have been known to tip over boats.

Our guide pointed out and named the water-birds. He even spotted a green snake camouflaged in a tree that overhung the river. He took us close so that we could see its skin. Luckily, this was not the venomous green mamba, but a much smaller harmless snake.

We had a magical evening, sitting outside around a roaring campfire. The stars sparkled above us. A tribesman entertained us with his re-tellings of some mythical stories from all over Africa, such as "The World Tree."

15

The World Tree

In the beginning, people and animals were created and lived together peacefully under the ground. They all spoke the same language. One day, the Creator built a new world with a giant tree, spreading out over the land, and laden with good things in its branches. He made a hole to bring the people and animals up to this new world. They were amazed. The Creator warned them not to make fire.

As the sun set, the people and animals all gathered beneath the tree. The people became colder and colder during the night. They shivered and were worried.

The people panicked and made a fire.
As they sat in the glow and warmth of
the flames, they turned happily to their
friends, the animals. But the animals
had fled, terrified of the fire.

   "Come back!" the people cried,
but the animals no longer understood
them and ran farther away.
The special friendship between
people and animals was broken.

Day 2

8:00 AM Breakfast

10:00 AM Waterhole watching

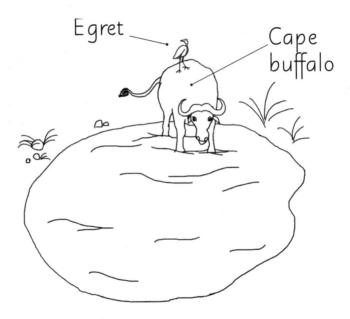

Egret

Cape buffalo

1:00 PM Lunch

3:30 PM Bush walk

7:00 PM Dinner and games

There is a waterhole in front
of our camp that we can see from
our tents. It has been busy with
animals visiting all morning.
I was very excited when a herd of
Cape buffalo came along to drink.
This is my first of the Big Five.

I used binoculars to take a closer look at the smaller birds. Some oxpeckers and cattle egrets perched on the backs of the buffalo. Every now and then, they pecked off a bug from the buffalo's skin. A busy weaver bird was collecting twigs. It wove them into its nest in a tree nearby.

Some silly vervet monkeys scampered along the wooden railings around our tent. We were told not to have food around. Now I know why! They were clever and fearless raiders. The troop was after anything they could find.

Before we set out on our afternoon bush walk, our guide gave a safety talk. He told us to stay close together and not to run. We also had to be quiet if the guide signaled with his hands.

A Maasai guide led at the front and our nature guide walked at the back of our group. We had only just started when we came upon a troop of baboons, relaxing on some rocks. Some of the younger ones were playing in the branches of the trees above them.

Animal tracks

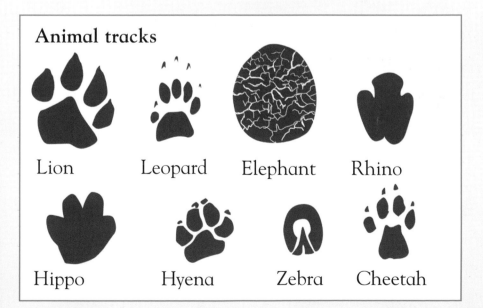

Lion   Leopard   Elephant   Rhino

Hippo   Hyena   Zebra   Cheetah

Most of the time we walked through the open grass areas. The grazing animals were always alert. I could understand why! The longer grass was a perfect hiding place for hunting animals. Lions and cheetahs could watch and wait for the right moment to leap into action.

On our way back to the camp, we had to keep very still as the troop of baboons strolled past. They were setting out to find food.

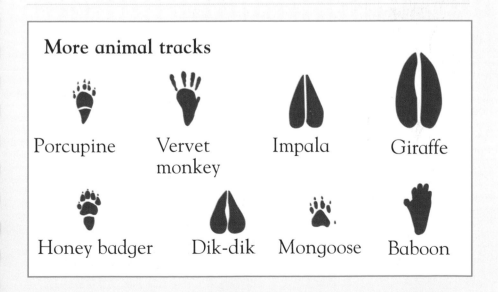

More animal tracks

Porcupine   Vervet monkey   Impala   Giraffe

Honey badger   Dik-dik   Mongoose   Baboon

Day 3

6:00 AM Breakfast

6:30 AM Radio tracking lions

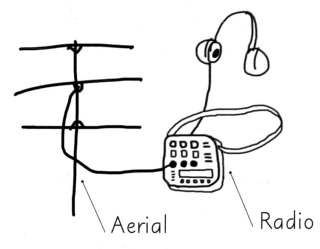

Aerial   Radio

12:00 noon Lunch

1:30 PM Visit Lake Nakuru

6:00 PM Preparing dinner

I have seen not just one lion but
a whole pride this morning! We
went out early with a research team
who monitor the lions in this area.
They have put a radio collar on
one of the females from each pride.
This helps the team find the prides.

The pride we followed this morning had three lionesses, eight cubs, and one large lion. The team could identify each lion by their whisker-spot pattern and had names for each one. We found the pride drinking by a small waterhole.

Whisker spots

King of cats
The lion is a social animal.
It is the largest and heaviest
of all the African big cats.
Its roar can carry 5 miles (8 km).

The lionesses were thirsty after
hunting during the nighttime.
The pride then found a cool place
in the shade to rest. The cubs
were very playful, though.

The team took pictures and
collected lion scat (poop) and hairs.
This was to help them collect
information about the pride.

    This afternoon, we drove to Lake Nakuru. The shoreline was a mass of pink. As we drove closer, we could make out thousands of flamingos. They were dipping their beaks to feed on the algae (water plants) in the warm water. The noise of all the birds was amazing. Every now and then, a few flamingos would take off. Their large black-edged wings flapped and their legs were stretched out behind.

    I wanted to stay longer, but we had to get back since we are cooking tonight. We will be making an African dish named Irio, which is potatoes and green vegetables mashed together.

Day 4

7:00 AM Breakfast

8:00 AM Waterhole watching

African elephant

1:00 PM Lunch

4:00 PM Rhino sanctuary

7:30 PM Dinner

I began the day by watching
the waterhole in front of our camp.

The herd of elephants had
arrived early for their first drink of
the day. There were eight adults
and two younger ones. The babies
were fun to watch as they played
in the water.

After bathing, the elephants sucked up dust into their trunks. They then sprayed the dust all over their bodies. Our guide told us that the dust acts as an insect repellent and also stops the sun from damaging their skin. We watched as the elephants tore up and ate grasses with their trunks. They would loosen some plants by kicking the roots with their front foot. They shook the dust off the roots before popping them into their mouths.

It is hard to imagine why these amazing giants are in danger from people.

This afternoon, I came face-to-face with another of the Big Five—the rhinos. They were magnificent. One of the black rhinos we saw had its horn removed. This would protect it from poachers. The number of rhinos was once very low in East Africa. However, a group of rhinos was brought to live in this large protected area.

Just before we left, we met Baraka, a blind black rhino. The rangers take care of him. Rhinos do not have very good eyesight, but a blind one would not survive in the wild.

Tracking rhinos
The research team uses helicopters to search for white rhinos in the park. The trackers aim to see each of the rhinos at least once every five days.

Day 5

7:30 AM Breakfast

9:00 AM Visit local village

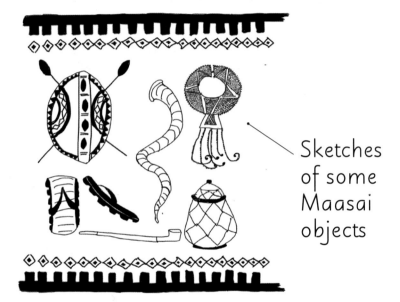

Sketches of some Maasai objects

1:00 PM Lunch
Afternoon free to rest and pack

6:00 PM Dinner

7:30 PM Night game drive

Our visit to a Maasai family began with the welcome jumping dance.

The tall Maasai warriors performed the dance. Their bodies were covered in red ochre (earth) and they jumped very high.

Around their homes, there is a circular fence known as the kraal. It is made from acacia thorns, which prevent lions from entering to attack the cattle, goats, and sheep.

This necklace was huge and colorful.

The cows are very important to the Maasai. They provide food, milk to drink, and are sold for money. The boys take them out to find grazing areas every day.

The women were dressed in bright, colored clothes and wore large, beaded necklaces. The beads were mainly red (the color of the Maasai), blue (the color of the sky), and green (the color of the grass). One woman showed us how they made their loaf-shaped homes. She used mud, sticks, grass, cow dung, and cow's urine.

Maasai Village

The Maasai are a group of people, or tribe, who live in Kenya and Tanzania. They have kept many of their old traditions.

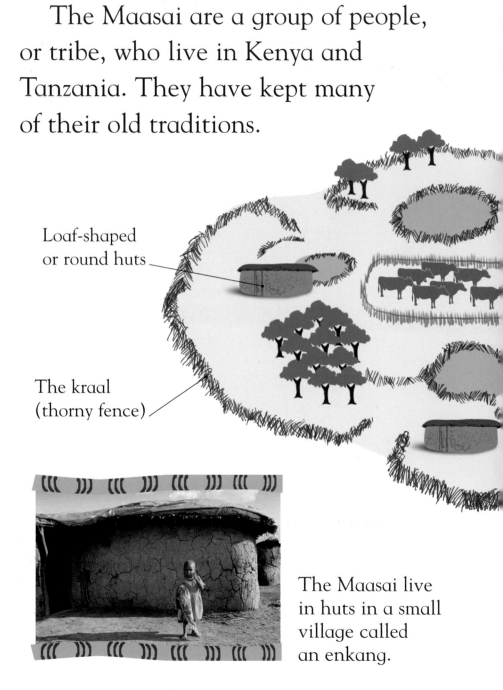

Loaf-shaped or round huts

The kraal (thorny fence)

The Maasai live in huts in a small village called an enkang.

It is dark and smoky inside the huts. The Maasai prepare meals on the fire. They mainly sleep on animal skins on the floor. They store fuel and keep small animals in the hut.

All animals are in the village at night.

Gaps in the fence are blocked at night.

A woman adding mud to the roof of her hut.

This evening's night drive was a wonderful end to our trip. The highlight was seeing the last of the Big Five—a leopard. In the glare of the spotlight, we watched it prowling through the bush. It was on its nightly hunt. Its glowing eyes stared straight at me.

The leopard watched us, too.

Animals behave differently at night. Hippos were out of the water, grazing on the riverbanks. We saw animals that would be asleep in their burrows during the day. The savannah was eerie but magical.

Glossary

Big Five
The five African animals that are considered the most dangerous.

Camouflage
Patterns and colors of skin that help animals to blend in with their surroundings.

Highlight
An interesting detail or event.

Migrating
Moving from one area to another.

Monitor
To watch and check over a period of time.

Myth
A legend, fable, or traditional story.

Poaching
Killing and stealing animals without permission.

Pride
A group of lions.

Repellent
A smell or liquid that keeps away pests.

Research
The study of materials and observations to find out facts.

Savannah
A large area of flat grassland with a few trees found in hot countries.

Tracking
Following the marks left behind by an animal.

Traditions
Stories, practices, and beliefs that are passed down from one generation to the next.

Tribesman
A member of the traditional hunting people.

Troop
A large group of animals, such as monkeys and apes.

Venomous
Able to pass on venom (poison) in a bite or a sting.

Waterhole
A hollow filled with water, forming a pool, that is used by animals as a bathing and drinking place.

Index

acacia thorns 39
African antelopes 10
algae (water plants) 30

baboon 22, 25
burrows 45

campfire 6, 14
Cape buffalo 5, 18, 19, 20
cattle 39
cattle egrets 18, 20
cows 41
cheetah 9, 23, 24
crocodiles 12

dik-dik 8, 11, 25

elephants 5, 23, 32, 33, 35
    trunks 35
enkang 42

flamingos 30

game drive 6, 7, 38
gazelle 8
gemsbok 11
gerenuk 10
giraffe 9, 25
greater kudu 11
guide 12, 14, 22

helicopter 37
hippos 12, 23, 45
    pods 12

honey badger 25
hyena 23

impala 9, 25
Irio 30

jeep 6, 9

Kenya 42
kraal 39, 42

Lake Nakuru 26, 30
leopard 5, 23, 44
lion 5, 23, 24, 27–29
    cubs 28, 29
    pride 27, 28, 29
    roar 29
    scat 29
    whisker spot 28

Maasai 22, 39, 41, 42–43
    homes 41
    hut 43
    necklaces 40, 41
marabou storks 5
migrating 8
mongoose 25
Mount Kenya 4
mythical stories 14
    The World Tree 14, 16–17

Nairobi 4

oxpeckers 20

poachers 36
porcupine 25

radio 26, 27
rangers 37
rhino 5, 23, 36–37
river 6
riverbanks 45

savannah 7, 10, 45
snake 14
    green mamba 14
    green snake 14

Tanzania 42
Thomson's gazelle 10
topi 10
tracks 23, 25
tribesman 14

vervet monkey 21, 25

water-birds 14
waterhole 18–19, 28, 32–33
weaver bird 20
wildebeest 8

zebra 8, 23

DK READERS help children learn to read, then read to learn. If you enjoyed this DK READER, then look out for these other titles ideal for your child.

Level 2 The Great Panda Tale

The zoo is getting ready to welcome a new panda baby. Join the excitement as Louise tells of her most amazing summer as a member of the zoo crew. What will the newborn panda look like?

Level 3 LEGO® Friends: Summer Adventures

Enjoy a summer of fun in Heartlake City with Emma, Mia, Andrea, Stephanie, Olivia, and friends.